Purely Italian
A COOKBOOK

BY CATERINA PAPADIA

TABLE OF CONTENTS

INTRODUCTION

PASTA (MAIN)
- Spaghetti Bolognese   10
- Risotto all Milanese   12
- Risotto agli Spinaci   14
- Pasta alla Norma   16
- Pizza Margherita   18
- Lasagne alla Bolognese   22
- Pasta e Fagioli   24
- Frittata di Spaghetti   26
- Farfalle al Salmone   28
- Pasta con Broccoli   30
- Pasta all'Amatriciana   32
- Pasta Gamberi & Piselli   34
- Linguine alla Genovese   36
- Pasta N'CAsciata   38
- Pasta con le Cozze   40

MAIN
- Spigola al acqua pazza   44
- Cotoletta alla Palermitana   46
- Polpette   48
- Braciole pugliesi   50
- Pollo alla caciatora   52
- Polenta salsiccia   54
- Sformato di zucchine   56
- Parmigiana   58
- Caponata Palermitana   60
- Ribollita Toscana   62

DESSERTS
- Torta Caprese   66
- Tiramisu   68
- Frittole di carnevale   70
- Crostata della nonna   72
- Crostatata di ricotta   74

INTRODUCTION

Welcome, or rather benvenuti, to this journey into Italian cuisine.

In Italy, food is the main topic of conversation (after football, for men).

In my experience, I've seen very few people in the world discussing food during dinner. This passion for eating well is widespread in the bel Paese. It's also the source of heated disputes between villages, which causes a lot of variety in some of the world's most renowned recipes.

Italian restaurants and Italian food have conquered the whole planet. However this incredible success has also led us to lose touch with traditional recipes, as they are still prepared in Italy.

This book is a celebration of Italian cuisine. As you will see, Italian food isn't hard to cook, allowing even a beginner to produce great meals with little effort.

ACKNOWLEDGEMENTS

I'd like to me thank Grandma' **Anna Rita** and my Mother-in-law for their support, teachings, little tricks and inspiration. Also, my wonderful husband, who has been my guinea pig all these years.

PASTA
(and Pizza)

Bolognese sauce is an original of Emilian cuisine that has become an icon of Italy. The sauce's preparation is easy, and it only takes time, care, and quality ingredients to perfect.

Outside Italy, the phrase Bolognese sauce is often used to describe any tomato sauce with minced meat - in Italy, it only represents a specific 'ragu', slow cooked and made in Bologna with a recipe that goes back to 1891. The meat needs to be simmered for a long time, so you'll have to be patient and let the meat cook, adding flavour to the sauce.

Because this recipe needs prolonged cooking, it's essential to choose a steel or cast-iron pot with a thick bottom, or a terracotta casserole dish.

Spaghetti Bolognese

Spaghetti Bolognese

Difficulty: *Medium*	Preparation: *Long*
Servings: *4-5*	Cost: *Medium*

INGREDIENTS

- 200g minced beef
- 150g minced pork
- 125g bacon in slices
- 350g tomato puree
- 50g carrots
- 50g golden onion
- 30g celery stick
- 100ml red wine
- 200g beef or vegetable stock
- 2 tbsp concentrated tomato puree
- 30g butter
- 4-5 tbsp. olive oil
- Salt
- Black pepper
- 400g pasta

INSTRUCTIONS

- Chop the bacon up fine.

- In a preheated saucepan, pour oil and add the pancetta, let it brown

- In the meantime, peel the carrots, then chop them finely with celery and onion

- As soon as the bacon is browned, add butter (let it melt first) and the chopped vegetables

- Stir and cook it on low heat for 5 minutes

- Add the minced meat and brown it over high heat, constantly stirring and breaking up meat with the back of a spoon

- Cook until the meat's no longer pink and lightly seared

- Wait until the meat is well browned before you pour in the wine

- It's important to seal the meat to prevent it from becoming tough or stringy during cooking

- Pour the wine and cook until the wine is reduced (when you no longer smell alcohol)

- Add the stock, salt and pepper to your taste.

- Stir in the puree, reduce the heat to a minimum and cover (don't close completely)

- Simmer for 2 hours, stirring from time to time

- You can start cooking the pasta or store the sauce in the fridge for 2-3 days, or freeze it when it's completely cool (once defrosted, simmer for 5 minutes before serving).

Risotto Milanese Style is a typical Milan's dish. It's known and loved throughout Italy and the world. Risotto's origin is found in Jewish and Arabic traditions. It became a signature dish of medieval Italian cuisine.

Risotto Alla Milanese was born in 1574, at the table of a Belgian glassmaker working on the Milan Cathedral. For his daughter's wedding, his colleagues added saffron and butter to a white risotto. Glassmakers used the spice to obtain a particular yellow colour of glass. The dish was immediately successful, both for its flavour and yellow hue, reminiscent of gold - synonymous with wealth. Saffron gave the recipe an unmistakable and robust aroma

Risotto alla Milanese

Risotto with Safron

Difficulty: *Easy*

Preparation: *Short*

Servings: *3*

Cost: *Low*

INGREDIENTS

- 300g Carnaroli rice
- 1 tsp (2g) saffron
- 60g butter
- 1 shallot
- 40ml white wine
- 50g Parmigiano or Grana Padano (grated)
- 1 litre of beef stock, or water
- Salt

robust flavour. If you want to get a lighter, more delicate taste, feel free to use just water.

- Halfway through cooking, add the saffron infuse and salt

- Once the risotto is cooked, remove it from the heat, stir in the grated cheese and the remaining butter

- Leave it for a couple of minutes before serving.

INSTRUCTIONS

- Put the pistils of saffron in a small glass and pour over some hot water

- Chop the shallot finely, so it melts during cooking

- In a large pan, melt half of the butter, add the shallot and simmer on a low heat till it softens.

- Add the rice and toast it over a high heat, constantly stirring for 3-4 minutes.

- Pour in the white wine and let it evaporate

- Cook the rice for about 18-20 minutes. Add the boiling stock (or water) a ladle at a time - it will be absorbed by the rice - stirring continuously.

- Traditionally, beef stock is used to get a rich and

This is a very simple but delicious recipe. A modern version of the Risotto family's version, it's particularly aromatic. Spinach makes it colourful, and if made in the season when fresh produce is available, it's particularly fragrant

Risotto con Spinaci

Risotto with Spinach

Difficulty: *Easy*	Preparation: *Short*
Servings: *3*	Cost: *Low*

INGREDIENTS

- 250g Carnaroli or Arborio rise
- 200g fresh or defrosted spinach (drained)
- 30g butter
- 1 shallot
- 40ml white wine
- 20-30g grated Parmigiano or Grana Padano
- 1-litre vegetable stock
- 1-2 tbsp olive oil
- Salt

- Stir well
- Serve immediately

INSTRUCTIONS

- Warm up the oil in a large pan, add the shallot and simmer on a low heat until it softens

- Add the rice and toast it over high heat, stirring for 3-4 minutes

- Pour in white wine and let it evaporate

- Cook the rice for about 18-20 minutes

- Add the boiling stock a ladle at a time – it'll be absorbed by the rice - stir continuously.

- When there's about 5 minutes left, add the spinach and salt

- Once the Risotto is ready, take it off the heat, add the butter and grated cheese.

Pasta with Aubergines, or as the Italian call it 'a *la Norma*', is the traditional pasta of Catania (Sicily). The name is connected to the Opera play of the same name written by Bellini. The recipe's Mediterranean taste made people call the dish a "Norma", meaning the best you can have. At that time, that's how Vincenzo Bellini's opera was considered. To prepare the original pasta recipe, you don't have to sing like a soprano - but you do need to use the right ingredients.

Pasta alla Norma

Pasta with Aubergines

Difficulty: *Medium*	Preparation: *Medium*
Servings: *3*	Cost: *Low*

INGREDIENTS

- 250g pasta (*rigatoni* is the best option)
- 350g tomato puree
- 2 medium aubergines
- half yellow onion
- 2 tbsp olive oil
- 3-4 fresh basil leaves
- Oil for frying
- Parmesan cheese to garnish at your taste
- Salt

INSTRUCTIONS

First, start prepare the tomato sauce:

- Warm up the saucepan, add the olive oil and finely chopped onion

- Brown the onion on a medium heat

- When it becomes golden in colour, pour the sauce in and 100 ml of water

- When it starts to boil, lower the heat and leave it to cook for about 15-20 minutes, stirring occasionally

- Add the basil and salt 5 minutes before the end of cooking

Now it's time for the rest of the dish:

- Peel the aubergines and cut them into 2-3 cm (1-inch) cubes

- Heat plenty of oil in a large pan (about 170c/ 338F) and fry the aubergines until they're a golden colour – do this a few at a time (you only need one layer of vegetables)

- Drain, and place them on absorbent paper to remove any excess oil

- Dust with a bit of salt.

- Once the sauce is ready, stir in all the fried aubergines and simmer for 5 minutes

- Boil the pasta in plenty of water, as indicated on the packer

- Drain the water and stir the pasta into the sauce.

- Serve the Pasta a la Norma with the dust of parmigiano

- Serve immediately

- If you want to stick to the tradition, though, you should swap parmigiano for salty ricotta, if you're lucky enough to find it in the store. It has a very delicate salty flavour.

- Enjoy the taste of Sicily!

Here It's in all its majesty - the pizza. It seems impossible that there was an era in which people could do without pizza. In 2017, Neapolitan pizza was granted world heritage status by UNESCO. The margherita, one of the most well-known foods in the world, was actually named after a real queen. The story goes that to honour Queen Margherita and the unification of Italy, in 1879, a Neapolitan pizzaiolo created the famous meal using tomato, mozzarella and basil to reflect the colours of the Italian flag.

INGREDIENTS

- 340g strong (bread) flour, plus some extra for dusting
- 240 ml warm water
- 3g dry yeast
- 5g salt

Weight scale

Pizza Margherita(1)
The DOUGH

Difficulty: *Medium*

Servings: *4*

Preparation: *Long*

Cost: *Low*

INSTRUCTIONS

- In a cup, melt the yeast with 100g of warm water (if you put your finger in the water, it should be warm, not hot). Leave till it a foam forms on the top

- In a mixing bowl, pour flour, salt and foaming yeast - you can use a stand mixer with a k-beater, or you can knead the dough in a traditional way – by hand

- In the beginning, use only about half of the water – add the water slowly while you're kneading

- The quantity of the water depends on the how absorbent the flour is, and the humidity of the room

- Work the dough until it's soft but compact

- Sprinkle the surface with a little bit of flour and scrape the dough out of the bowl onto the countertop

- Use a counter or tabletop that allows you to extend your arms to knead the dough, while not making you hunch over a table

- Start kneading the dough by pushing it down and then outward, only using the heels of your hands. Fold the dough in half toward you and press down. Turn the dough about 45 degrees and knead again with the heels of your hands, If it gets sticky, add a little more flour

- Continue to knead, folding and turning the dough until It's smooth and supple

- Place the dough in a large bowl (the dough will double in size, so pick a big enough bowl)

- Cover with the cling film and leave to prove

- The dough likes to be sheltered in a draughty and warm place

- Leave it until it doubles in size (this usually takes about 1-2 hours)

- Once the dough has doubled in size, place it on the worktop, dusted with flour, and knead it to deflate

- Cut off 260-280 grams using a weighing scale

- Form loaves by rolling them in your hands and closing them at the base

- Put them on a large tray with 10cm (4 inches) between each piece

- Cover loaves with cling film for the next stage of leavening and place them again in a warm place to prove

INGREDIENTS

PIZZA MARGHERITA

- 8 tbsp puree or blended peeled tomatoes
- 200g mozzarella
- Fresh basil leaves
- Olive Oil to garnish

Pizza Margherita(2)

The Pizza

Difficulty: *Medium*	Preparation: *Long*
Servings: *4*	Cost: *Medium*

INSTRUCTIONS (CONT'D)

- When the dough has raised again, remove the cling film and preheat the oven at 220C/428F. It is important that the oven has the right temperature and that the heat comes from the bottom to create the perfect crust

- Pour plenty of flour on the worktop

- Take a loaf, place it in the middle of the flour, so it doesn't stick to your hands or the work surface

- If you've ever seen a pizza-maker hit the dough with a small slap, they are doing so to give pizza a round shape – so do that too

- Starting from the dough's centre, push the air outwards by moving the fingers gently towards the edge

- With a rotating movement, widen the dough, which should take the shape of a disc

- Try to stretch the dough and not roll it out with a rolling pin (rolling removes all the bubbles from the pizza)

- Place it on the tray (round pizza tray if you have). Spread the tomato puree and chopped mozzarella.

- Put the Pizza in the oven on the lowest shelf.

- If you don't see creating the crust, place the tray directly on the oven's bottom (only if it's an electric oven), taking care not to burn it. Check constantly after the first 30 seconds; it won't take long.

- A quicker solution to the "crust issue" is to use a Pizza Stone or a Baking stone (or even a simple Tile can do) to help creating the crust. If you do not have those tools, you can follow our procedure, the results are outstanding as well.

- Check constantly after the first 30 seconds

- In total, cook the pizza for about 10 minutes and garnish it with fresh basil and a drizzle of oil

- Cook pizzas one at a time

- Margarita pizza is the basic Pizza. You can add any ingredient that you like.

-

Lasagna is one of the most well-known pasta dishes in the whole world. It's been on Italian tables since the 19th century. It's the typical main course of many Italian celebrations. Lasagne has had a lot of different variants throughout the centuries. You can find a vegetarian lasagna with zucchini, or a more creative pumpkin and gorgonzola version. You can also push yourself to experiment with lasagne with fish.

Lasagna is a very versatile pasta. Still, you risk angering your Italian guests if you don't prepare a proper lasagne with ragu for Christmas.

INGREDIENTS

FOR RAGU' (MEAT SAUCE)

- 500g (400g dry lasagne pasta) fresh lasagne pasta
- 400g minced beef
- 150g minced pork
- 400g tomato puree
- 1 carrot
- 1 medium yellow onion
- 1 celery stick
- 100 ml red wine
- 300-400ml beef, chicken or vegetable stock
- 4-5 tbsp olive oil
- 1 bay leaf
- Salt
- Black pepper
- 60g grated Parmigiano or Grana Padano
- 40g butter

FOR THE BECHAMEL SAUCE:

- 750ml full fat milk
- 75g plain flour
- 75g butter
- Salt
- A pinch of nutmeg

Lasagne al Ragù *(Bolognese)*

Lasagne with meat sauce

Difficulty: *Medium*	Preparation: *Long*
Servings: *5-6*	Cost: *Medium*

INSTRUCTIONS

- Chop the vegetables into small cubes of the same size. Heat the olive oil in a souse pan and stir in and cook the vegetables on low heat for about 5 minutes.

- Add the minced meat, brown it over high heat, constantly stirring and breaking up meat with the back of a spoon.

- Cook until no longer pink and lightly seared. When the meat is well browned, pour in the wine. It's important to seal well the meat to prevent it from becoming tough or stringy during prolonged cooking.

- Pour the wine and cook until wine is mainly reduced (when you no longer smell alcohol). Add the stock, bay leaf, salt and pepper to your taste.

- Stir in tomato puree, reduce the heat to a minimum and cover the saucepan with the lid, but don't close completely. Now simmer it for about 2 hours, continuously stirring from time to time.

- In a small saucepan, heat the butter and melt it over low heat. Add the flour a little at a time, stirring constantly and keeping the heat low.

- Add the hot milk, continuing to stir as you go, until you get a smooth sauce. Add salt, pepper and nutmeg to your taste. Cook for a couple of minutes, stirring continuously until the sauce has thickened.

- If you use a dry lasagne sheet, add 100 ml of milk in the cooked bechamel souse as the dry Pasta will absorb more liquid.

- Once the ragu is done and cooked, you can start to assemble the Lasagne.

- Preheat the oven at 190 C or 374 F.

- Spread a little ragu onto the lasagne dish or roasting pan. Lay the first layer of lasagne sheets, breaking any as necessary to fit.

- Everything should be covered (don't overlap as the Pasta will widen while cooking). Pour a ladle or more of ragu on the lasagne sheet (paying attention to cover the surface evenly and abundantly), then bechamel sauce on the top. Add more layers until all the ingredients are used up. In case you are using freshly made lasagna, pierce with a fork each sheet as you go. In the last layer, mix a little ragu together with the bechamel sauce. To form an exceptional crust, always use grated Parmesan cheese and many flakes of butter.

- Lasagne must cook at 190 degrees for 20-30 minutes. The important thing is constantly checking that the Pasta does not burn on the surface but is soft and cooked inside.

- If you notice that the top starts to get brown, but the inside is still not done, cover the dish with foil, then check in 5 minutes.

- Let settle the Lasagne for about 10 minutes before serving.

After Italians started settling in America, pasta fasul became the symbol of Italian food in the States. It's not a fancy pasta, but It's very versatile and works with a wide variety of ingredients. The texture can vary from soupy to dense, but if it's cooked well, any spoon brings with it lots of flavour.

Pasta e Fagioli

Pasta with Beans

Difficulty: *Low*	Preparation: *Short*
Servings: *3*	Cost: *Low*

INGREDIENTS

- 120g pasta ditalini or other small, short pasta
- 250g dry barlotti beans - about 2.5 tins (400g)
- 200g tomato puree or any small tomatoes
- Half a carrot
- Half an onion
- 1 garlic clove
- 1 bay leaf
- A pinch of rosemary
- Salt
- Olive oil to serve

INSTRUCTIONS

- Soak the beans in water overnight

- Rinse them, transfer them into a saucepan, and cover them with cold water (1-2 cm over the beans' level)

- Add the bay leaf, garlic, rosemary, chopped carrot and onion and tomato puree

- Bring to the boil and simmer on a low heat for 70-80 minutes, stirring occasionally. If the water has evaporated too much, add more

- After one hour, add the salt and black pepper and remove the bay leaf.

- Once ready, take 1/3 of the beans and blend with a blender

- Pour it into the mixture and stir

- Now you can add cooked pasta to the beans

- Serve with some olive oil

This clever idea of cooking leftover pasta and adding simple ingredients like eggs, cheese and pepper, was born in Naples.

It's thought to date back to post-war time. During this period, the food supply was limited, especially in the South of Italy, and cutlery was a luxury item. Neapolitans invented a way of using pasta leftovers and creating a recipe that can be eaten on the go, without cutlery. The frittata di spaghetti (or any other pasta, such as macarino) was made to be shared at the table and sliced into a portion, like a cake. This dish is all about creativity, so don't be afraid to experiment by using this as the starting point. Once you've added eggs and cheese, you can try anything. Don't worry - it can't go wrong!

Frittata di Spaghetti

Spaghetti Omelette

Difficulty: *Medium*	Preparation: *Medium*
Servings: *4-5*	Cost: *Low*

INGREDIENTS

- 350g Spaghetti
- 5 eggs
- 50g parmesan or grana padano grated
- 100g scamorza (provola or mozzarella)
- 100g pancetta cubes
- 20g butter
- Black pepper
- Salt
- 2-3 tbsp oil
- Non-stick pan 24-26 cm / 10 inch

INSTRUCTIONS

- Cook the spaghetti al dente (or use leftovers)

- In a large bowl, mix the eggs, parmesan, scamorza, pancetta, butter (cut into small pieces), salt and pepper.

- Heat the oil in the non-stick pan, then pour the mixture into the pan

- Let it cook over low heat for 10-15 minutes with a lid

- Lift the omelette a bit carefully to check if a crust has formed on the bottom - iIt should have a nice golden colour

- Place the omelette on a large plate so that the crust is on the top

- Heat another spoon of oil in the pan

- Slide the omelette from the uncooked side into the pan

- Cook for about 5 minutes without a lid, until a golden crust has formed on the other side

- Let it cool before cutting. It's delicious either warm or cold, and ideal for taking on picnice

- For the preparation of the pasta omelette, you can vary the ingredients by using cooked ham, salami or frankfurters instead of pancetta and replacing the scamorza with mozzarella, smoked provola, emmental or mild cedar etc.

This elegant and gentle pasta dish encapsulates all the joys of Italian cooking.

Italian cuisine can be luxurious, delicious and full of flavour by using just three ingredients (give or take).

When you taste a portion of pasta with salmon, the only thing you ask is just how come a simple dish like this can taste like heaven. Give it a try, and see for yourself how easy it is to create such a masterpiece.

Farfalle al Salmone

Pasta with Salmon

Difficulty: *Low*	Preparation: *Short*
Servings: *3*	Cost: *Medium*

INGREDIENTS

- 300g pasta Farfalle
- 150g smoked Salmon
- 180g single cream
- 1 clove garlic
- Black pepper
- Salt
- 3 tbsp olive oil

INSTRUCTIONS

- First of all, start to cook the pasta

- Farfalle is the classic choice, but penne or rigatoni will work as well

- Cut the smoked salmon into cubes

- Heat the oil in a pan and brown the garlic

- Cook half of the salmon for a couple of minutes on medium heat.

- Pour the single cream, stir for a minute adding the other half of the salmon and remove the pan from the heat

- Take out the garlic

- Drain the pasta (that should be ready by this time) but leave aside a cupful for cooking water (you may need it if you find the pasta a bit dry)

- Add the cooked pasta and black pepper to the sauce, mix and season

- Turn the heat back on and mix everything together

- Serve immediately

Probably one of the most famous pasta dishes from Puglia is o*recchiette con cime di rapa (Turnip tops)* - a vegetable that is very difficult to find and that is not only very seasonal but also not easy to cut and clean.

New generations are less inclined to spend so much time preparing, so they've recreated the original dish's taste using a more familiar and consistent vegetable: broccoli.

It doesn't taste the same, but it's very similar and undoubtedly more kid friendly than the original (Turnip tops have a subtle, bitter aftertaste that not everyone loves). If you want a taste of Puglia, without the adventure of finding and cleaning *cime di rapa*, pasta con broccoli is the answer.

Pasta con Broccoli

Pasta with Broccoli

Difficulty: *Low*	Preparation: *Short*
Servings: *2-3*	Cost: *Low*

INGREDIENTS

- 175g pasta
- 1 medium broccoli
- 1 garlic clove
- 2 anchovies in oil
- 1 chilli paper
- 3 tbsp olive oil
- Salt

INSTRUCTIONS

- Wash the broccoli

- Cut the florets to the same size

- Boil the broccoli in salted water. When cooked, drain and set aside

- Keep the cooking water

- In the meantime, cook the pasta

- Heat the oil in the pan, add garlic, chilli and anchovies, making them melt over medium heat

- Remove the chilli; if you like a very hot spicy taste, leave it till the end.

- Add the broccoli, crush it, pour a bit of the broccoli's cooking water to create a soft mixture

- Season with salt, cover and let the broccoli sit for a couple of minutes

- Drain the pasta and add it to the broccoli. Stir well.

- Garnish with olive oil and grated parmesan to your taste (to be honest there is no parmesan in the origina recipe, but my kids love it!)

- Serve immediately

Originating from the town of Amatrice (in the province of Rieti, not far from Rome), the amatriciana is one of the best known pasta sauces in present day Roman and Italian cuisine.

This pasta has been named a traditional agro-alimentary product of Lazio by the Italian government. The dish is confirmation that you don't need many ingredients to create an incredibly tasteful dish. Simplicity is key.

Spaghetti all'Amatriciana

Pasta all'Amatriciana

Difficulty: *Medium*

Servings: *3*

Preparation: *Medium*

Cost: *Medium*

INGREDIENTS

- 240g Pasta
- 300g guanciale or pancetta
- 500-600g chopped tomatoes or puree
- 80g Pecorino gated
- 50 ml White vine
- 1 chilli pepper
- Salt
- Olive oil

- Serve immediately

- Did you think impressing your guests with one of the most iconic Italian dishes was too difficult? Well.....think again.

INSTRUCTIONS

- Heat 1 tbsp of olive oil and add the chilli

- Cut the guanciale (or bacon) into stripes.

- Brown the bacon until it has browned, then pour white wine and let it evaporate

- Drain the bacon, remove the chilli and set aside

- Add the chopped tomatoes into the same pan, continue cooking the sauce for about 10 minutes.

- Start cooking the spaghetti until cooked al dente.

- Once the tomato sauce is cooked, add the bacon to the pan, taste for seasoning and let it cook for a couple of minutes

- Add the spaghetti, pecorino and mix it all together

Italy is blessed not only with beautiful coastline, but also by ancient mountains. So many recipes are a mixture of these two natural beauties. Pasta with prawns and peas fuse the taste of the sea with the taste of the countryside.

Pasta Gamberi & Piselli

Pasta with Prawn and Peas

Difficulty: *Medium*	Preparation: *Medium*
Servings: *4-5*	Cost: *Medium*

INGREDIENTS

- 400g pasta
- 480g prawns
- 400g frozen peas
- 1 garlic clove
- Half a yellow onion
- 2- 3 sprigs of parsley
- Olive oil

INSTRUCTIONS

- In a saucepan, heat 2 tbsp of oil on a medium heat

- Add finely chopped onion and cook until golden

- Add the peas and cover with 1-2 cm (half an inch) of hot water

- Cover and simmer on a low heat for about 15 minutes until soft

- Boil water for the pasta, add salt to taste

- Start cooking the pasta

- In a pan, heat the 1-2 tbsp of oil and brown the garlic

- Fry the prawns little at the time - cover the bottom of the pan with prawns and cook on a medium-high heat, sprinkling with salt

- When the prawns becomes pink on one side, turn them and cook for about 1 minute

- Remove the prawns and put aside, sprinkle with chopped parsley

- The pasta should be ready now

- Drain it, remembering to leave aside some cooking water that can be used if you find your sauce a bit dry

- Blend 2/3 of peas to a smooth puree.

- Put it all together in the pan that you used to cook the pasta, and mix

- Serve immediately

This incredibly green pasta is a classic of Ligurian cuisine.

Pesto will delight you with the unmistakable aroma of basil. The addition of potatoes and green beans makes this dish unique, memorable, and tasty, which will conquer many people, especially vegetarians and vegans.

Linguine alla Genovese

Linguine with Pesto Potatoes and Green Beans

Difficulty: *Medium*

Servings: *4-5*

Preparation: *Medium*

Cost: *Low*

INGREDIENTS

- 300g linguine
- 350g potatoes
- 250g green beans trimmed
- Pesto already made
- Olive oil
-

Ingredients for pesto (in case you would like to make your own):

-
- 50g fresh basil leaves
- Half a clove of garlic
- 50g grated Parmesan or Grana Padano 100 g Olive oil
- 60g pine nuts

INSTRUCTIONS

- The original recipe uses linguine, but you can use any kind of pasta you like

- In case you would like to make your own pesto, you will need a pestle and mortar or blender

- If you use a blender, place the blender blades in the freezer to prevent them from overheating while blending (doing this will allow you to preserve the brilliant colour of the basil)

- Place a large pot with plenty of water on the heat, and add salt

- Peel the potatoes, cut them into thick cubes of 2-3 cm (1 inch) on each side.

- Add the potatoes to the water

- Cut the green beans in half and put them into the same pot

- 2 minutes later, add the linguine and cook for the time indicated on the packet

- Prepare the pesto. Put the cold blades in the blender, then pour the basil leaves (clean but not washed to avoid the risk of them spoiling)

- Add a clove of peeled garlic, parmesan and pecorinol, pine nuts and salt

- Blend with small pauses to prevent the blades over-heating, or use the "pulse" function

- The basil leaves should return a nice brilliant green colour. While the blades are in operation, pour the olive oil slowly from the spout of the lid

- By this time, the pasta and vegetables should be ready. Drain them, remembering to keep aside cooking water in a cup

- Put everything back in the same pot and add pesto. Mix. Add a bit of cooking water if you find your pasta a bit dry

This baked Pasta is a real triumph. It's a Sicilian extravaganza, a dish that must be shared with family or friends, It's the Inspector Montalbano's favourite pasta, the TV character adapted from Andrea Camilleri's novels.

If you manage to save some pasta for the next day, it will be even tastier

INGREDIENTS

For the sauce:
- 500g beef mince
- 700g tomato puree
- 1 medium yellow onion
- 1 medium carrot
- 1 celery stick
- 100 ml white wine
- 2-3 tbsp olive oil
- Fresh basil leaves

For the pasta:
- 500g rigatoni pasta
- 2 medium eggplants
- Frying oil
- 150g cooked ham
- 150g mozzarella
- 100g provola or scamorsa (semi-soft cow's milk cheese)
- 50g parmesan
- 3 eggs

Pasta N' Casciata

Detective Montalbano's Pasta

Difficulty: **High**

Servings: **6-7**

Preparation: **Long**

Cost: **Medium**

INSTRUCTIONS

First, start with the preparation of the tomato sauce

Finely chop the vegetables

Heat the olive oil in a casserole dish, cook the vegetables on low heat for about 5 minutes

Add the minced meat, brown it over high heat, constantly stirring and breaking up the meat with the back of a spoon

Cook until no longer pink and lightly seared. Wait until the meat is well browned before you pour in the wine

Pour the wine and cook for about 2-3 minutes (when you no longer smell alcohol)

Stir in tomato puree, basil leaves and 300ml of water, reduce the heat to let it bubble lightly

Cook with no lid for 30 minutes, stirring from time to time

Add salt when it's ready.

Peel the aubergines and cut them into 2-3 cm (1-inch) cubes or slices

Heat plenty of oil in a large pan (about 170 C or 338 F) and fry the aubergines until they're golden a few at a time

Drain and place the aubergines on absorbent paper to remove excess oil and dust with a bit of salt.

Make hard-boiled eggs

Boil pasta in salted water for 10 minutes. Drain it

Once all the ingredients are cooked, you ready to assemble the Montalbano's Pasta

In a big bowl, mix the boiled pasta, fried eggplants, sauce, parmesan

Cut the the mozzarella, provola and ham into cubes. If you couldn't find provola or scamorza, use mozzarella instead (250g in total)

Oil an oven-safe baking dish, place half of the pasta mixture in it, slice the boiled egg and lay it over the top

Top with the remaining pasta.

Put it in a preheated oven at 180 C (360 F) on the middle shelf, and cook for 20-25 minutes to create a golden crust on top

Leave to cook for 10-15 minutes

Enjoy!

The easiest way to dive into the Mediterranean sea, savouring all the flavours it can offer.

The secrets of this dish are the quality of the raw ingredients and its simplicity. The balance of the different flavours makes this recipe at the same time unique, delicate and modern but with traditional roots.

Pasta con le Cozze
Pasta with Mussels

Difficulty: *Medium*	Preparation: *Short*
Servings: *3*	Cost: *Medium*

INGREDIENTS

- 300g spaghetti or linguine
- 500g fresh mussels
- 1 garlic clove
- 10 baby plum or cherry tomatoes
- 3-4 tbsp olive oil
- Parsley
- Salt
- Chilli oil or chilli powder (optional)

INSTRUCTIONS

- Remove all broken or damaged mussels

- If some shells are open try to touch the inside with a knife, if the shell close the mollusc is alive (and can be cooked safely) if not is better not to use that shell.

- Wash them under cold water, drain and put them aside in a bowl

- Boil them in salted water, in a stockpot

- Cook the pasta for the time indicated on the package

- Heat the pan over medium-high heat

- Brown the garlic, cut the tomatoes in half, put them in with the garlic and sprinkle over some salt

- Add the mussels, cover and cook for 1-2 minutes after sprinkling with parsley

- As soon the shells start to open, stir and cover again with the lid

- The mussels are done when they are detached from the shell

- By this time, the spaghetti should be ready

- Drain well but remember to put aside a cup of the cooking water

- In case the pasta is too dry, add cooking water to make it smooth and creamy

- Add the pasta to the mussels, stir well. Remove the garlic

- Serve with a dust of chopped parsley and chilli (if required)

- Serve immediately

MAIN

Sea bass in "crazy water" is one of the simplest and most delicious ways to cook fish.

This way of preparing sea bass is the perfect way to taste the authentic flavour of the Mediterranean, without requiring too much in terms of ingredients and preparation.

Spigola all'acquapazza

Sea Brass cooked in "crazy water"

Difficulty: *Medium*	Preparation: *Medium*
Servings: **2**	Cost: *High*

INGREDIENTS

- 300g - 400g of sea bass (2 fillets)
- 10-15 baby plum tomatoes
- 50ml white wine
- 1 garlic clove
- 3-4 tbsp olive oil
- Salt
- Large pan
- Parsley

Large pan (to fit 2 fishes)

INSTRUCTIONS

- Ensure the fish is clean by washing it and wiping it with a paper towel

- Use a dull knife or a spoon to remove the scales

- Work against the average direction of the scales, raking up from tail to head. It helps to remove the scales under running water or simply underwater in the sink, to prevent a mess

- From the base of the gills, make a shallow cut with a sharp knife along the fish's belly, stopping at the end

- Use your fingers or a spoon to scoop out the fish's innards. Rewash it and wipe

- Heat the oil in a large pan on medium-high heat. Brown the garlic and add half cut baby tomatoes. Cook for 1 minute

- Place the fish in between the tomatoes

- Fry for 2 minutes and add wine

- Cook until the alcohol evaporates

- Cover half of the fish with water

- Sprinkle with salt and finely chopped parsley.

- Cover, and leave to cook for 10-15 minutes at a medium-low heat (cooking times vary depending on the size of the fish). Keep basting the fish with sauce

- Remove the lid and raise the heat

- Cook for another 3-5 minutes, basting the fish with sauce. Let thicken the sauce.

- Enjoy the taste of the sea

Sicilian cuisine is known for frying anything that can be put in a pan - calamari, auberginesor rice (arancini). It's surprising to discover that the local version of the very famous cotoletta alla milanese - the palermo style cutlet - takes a fried classic of the Italian tradition and transforms it into a baked version.

The breadcrumbs are often mixed with parsley and pecorino cheese. Unlike the Milanese cutlet, the Palermitana cutlet doesn't contain eggs. It can be done using veal, as in the original version, but also with beef or chicken

Cotoletta alla Palermitana

Palermo style 'cutlet'

Difficulty: *Medium*	Preparation: *Medium*
Servings: *2-3*	Cost: *Medium*

INGREDIENTS

- 500g chicken breast
- 100g breadcrumbs
- 25g parmesan (grated)
- half garlic clove (optional)
- 1-2 sprigs of parsley
- Black pepper
- Salt
- Olive oil 70-80ml
- Lemon juice to sprinkle (optional)

INSTRUCTIONS

- With a sharp knife, cut the chicken breast into slices of about 1 centimetre

- Tenderise the chicken with a mallet

- If you prefer, you can use beef, choosing the most tender slices such as rump

- Finely chop 1/2 clove of garlic and mix it with breadcrumbs, parmesan and chopped fresh parsley

- Season to taste, then mix well

- Place the mixture onto a large plate

- On another plate or bowl, pour olive oil

- Dip each slice into the oil and coat each side in the breadcrumb's mixture (be generous with the olive oil, it acts as a glue between the meat and the breading)

- Place the breaded slices onto a baking tray lined with baking paper

- Preheat the oven to 180 C (360F) and place the tray on the middle shelf for about 10 minutes (depending on the slice's thickness). Bake until golden and cooked through.

- (Optional) Before serving, pour over some lemon juice

- The dish is ready

Polpette, or meatballs, are the cornerstone of any Italian family culinary tradition.

There is not one correct way of preparing them, but I would say there are as many ways as many Italian families exist in the world. It's amazing to see how many variations an dish like this can have - from the kind of meat used, to the percentage of bread and the type of bread used in the mix, the number of eggs to the way of preparing the meatballs. The results are always delicious. You can develop your own version or use the one we use in our family.

Polpette al sugo di Nonna

Grandma's meatballs with tomato sauce

Difficulty: *Medium*	Preparation: *Medium*
Servings: *4-5*	Cost: *Low*

INGREDIENTS

For meat balls:

- 500g beef mince
- 60g breadcrumbs
- 30g grated parmesan or grana padano cheese
- 2 eggs
- 1/2 garlic clove
- 2-3 sprigs of parsley
- Salt
- Olive oil to fry
- 680g-700g tomato puree
- Half a medium onion
- Some fresh basil leaves
- 2 tbsp olive oil

INSTRUCTIONS

- In a large saucepan, chop a brown onion with oil, add the puree, basil leaves and simmer on medium heat for about 10 minutes. Add salt

- Put mince, breadcrumbs, parmesan or grana padano, eggs, finely grated garlic, salt and chopped parsley in a bowl

- Mix everything with your hands until soft

- Add water little by little

- Wet hands with water to prevent the meatballs sticking to all surfaces.

- Make the meatballs by rolling a full teaspoon of the mixture between your hands.

- Once the meatballs are ready, preheat the oil in a pan and brown the meatballs on all sides for a couple of minutes

- Put the fried meatballs in a saucepan with sauce, and cook on a low-medium heat for 15- 20 minutes

- You can cook some pasta alongside it if you want to.

- Before serving, sprinkle with grated parmesan cheese

Beef chops with sauce are among the most popular dishes of the Bari culinary tradition. These are beef rolls (even if the original Bari recipe calls for horse meat) with a filling of parsley, garlic and pecorino simmered in tomato sauce. This delicacy can be enjoyed on bread, accompanied by a fresh salad or baked potatoes. The sauce can also season the orecchiette (short pasta), just like It's done in Puglia..

Braciole Pugliesi

Apulian beef chops

Difficulty: *High*	Preparation: *Long*
Servings: *3-4*	Cost: *Medium*

INGREDIENTS

- 750g thin beef slices
- 680g-700g tomato puree
- Half a yellow medium onion
- 50-60 g pecorino grated
- 100ml white wine
- 1 garlic clove
- 3-4 sprigs of parsley
- 2-3 tbsp olive oil
- Salt

INSTRUCTIONS

- Tenderise the beef with a mallet - make the slices no higher than 2-3 mm (1/8 inch).

- Finely chop the parsley and the garlic

- Put a teaspoon of parsley, garlic mix and half tsp of grated Pecorino on each slice of beef

- Roll up the pieces of meat to form small rolls (you can use toothpicks or a string to close the rolls - just remember to remove it before serving)

- Heat the oil on a medium to high heat in a casserole dish

- Finely chop the onion and add it to the pan with the meat rolls

- Brown the rolls on both sides.

- Pour in the wine and cook until it evaporates

- Add the puree and about 300 ml of water

- Bring to a boil, reduce the heat, cover and simmer for about 2-3 hours, stirring occasionally

- Add the salt at the end of the cooking

- Chops are ready to be served

This recipe originated during the Renaissance. Pollo alla cacciatora (Hunter's style chicken) combines three very rich ingredients: chicken, spices (expensive for the period) and an ingredient that would soon dominate Italian cuisine, but was rare at the time - the tomato

Pollo alla Cacciatora

Chicken 'Hunter' Style

Difficulty: *Medium*

Servings: *3-4*

Preparation: *Shor*

Cost: *Low*

INGREDIENTS

- 750g chicken (thighs or drumsticks)
- Half a yellow onion
- Half a carrot
- 1 garlic clove
- 10-15 olives
- 50ml white wine
- 200g chopped or peeled tomatoes
- Sage
- Rosemary
- Parsley to garnish

INSTRUCTIONS

- Finely chop the carrot, onion and garlic

- Put the chicken into a casserole dish and brown on each side

- Add the vegetables and herbs. Cook for 2 minutes

- Pour in the wine and cook for 2-3 minutes, until the alcohol is evaporated

- Add the tomatoes, olives and 100g of water

- Simmer with the lid on, until the chicken is cooked, adding the salt halfway in

This dish is very famous in the northern part of Italy, prepared and enjoyed mainly in the cold winter months. A very easy recipe to prepare, but rich in flavour.

Polenta con Salsiccia

Polenta with sausages

Difficulty: *Easy*

Servings: *4*

Preparation: *Short*

Cost: *Medium*

INGREDIENTS

- 200g pre-cooked polenta
- 50g butter
- 50g grated parmesan or grana padano cheese
- 500g sausage (100% pork meat)
- 1 garlic clove
- 100g white wine
- 1 tbsp olive oil
- Salt
- Water for polenta check the instructions on the package

INSTRUCTIONS

- Separate the sausages by cutting them, if they're still connected in a row

- In a pan large enough to fit all sausages in one layer, pour in the oil and heat it on medium heat

- Put in the garlic and the sausages

- When the sausages and garlic start to brown, add the wine

- Cook for about 2-3 minutes, until the alcohol has evaporated

- Turn the sausages over, reduce the heat and cover

- Cook for about 5-10 minutes (depending on the sausages' thickness)

- Make sure the liquid doesn't totally evaporate

- While the sausages are cooking, prepare the polenta

- Boil some water (usually you need 200ml for every 50g of pre-cooked polenta)

- Gradually add the polenta to the boiling water, stirring continuously

- Bring back to the boil and simmer for a couple of minutes on a low heat

- Add grated cheese and butter, season with salt

- Serve the polenta topped with sausages and gravy. Sprinkle some parmesan if required

- Serve immediately

One of the best ways to feed your kids, with this fantastic and healthy vegetable dish. The recipe is extremely simple, and extremely tasty. Your kids will love it, and the grown-ups will ask for the recipe.

Sformato di zucchine

Courgettes Flan

Difficulty: *Easy*

Servings: *4*

Preparation: *Short*

Cost: *Medium*

INGREDIENTS

- 500g courgettes
- 2 eggs
- 250g ricotta
- 50g breadcrumbs
- 30g parmesan or grana padano
- 100g mild cheddar, edam or any cheese suitable for melting
- Salt
- Handful of breadcrumbs

INSTRUCTIONS

- Grate the courgettes, and squeeze off any excess juice

- Place the courgettes in a large bowl. Add the eggs, ricotta, breadcrumbs, parmesan, grated cheese and salt. Mix well. You also can add pieces of cooked ham or smoked cheese.

- Preheat the oven to 200C (390 F)

- Spread a handful of breadcrumbs in an oven-safe, oiled dish

- Pour in the mixture. Sprinkle some olive oil and breadcrumbs over the top

- Bake for 20-25 minutes. If it starts to brown too much, cover the dish with aluminium foil

- When it's ready, let it cool for 10 minutes

- Serve immediately

The eggplant *parmigiana* is a major dish of Italian culinary tradition, but parmigiana is loved not only in Italy but all over the world. The original recipe is disputed between the regions of southern Italy but the dish is a symbol of Mediterranean cuisine.

Parmigiana di Melanzane
Aubergine Parmigiana

Difficulty: *High*

Preparation: *Long*

Servings: *4*

Cost: *Medium*

INGREDIENTS

- 750g eggplants
- 680g-700g tomato puree or blended peeled tomatoes
- Half medium golden onion
- 300g mozzarella
- 60g parmesan
- 1 tbsp olive oil
- 2-3 fresh basil leaves
- Oil to fry
- Salt

INSTRUCTIONS

- Peel aubergines and cut off the stalks

- Slice lengthwise in 4-5 mm (1/3 inch) slices

- Pour water into a large bowl and add plenty of salt

- Add the aubergine and cover with water

- Leave for half an hour. Salt, in this case, will eliminate the stingy taste from eggplants and give a nice golden colour when you fry it

- Finely cope the onions. Heat the olive oil in a saucepan and fry the onions until browned

- Add the puree, 200ml of water and basil leaves

- Simmer the sauce for 30 minutes. Season to taste

- Start frying the eggplants until they get to a golden colour

- Drain, squeeze off any excess water and put them onto kitchen towels

- Stand them on the kitchen towels.

- Heat the oil in a pan

- Place the eggplant slices carefully into the oil next to each other. Fry them one layer at a time

- Once golden, remove the slices and set them on the kitchen towel to absorb the excess oil.

- Take an oven-safe dish (20 x 20cm)

- Spread a bit of sauce on the bottom. Form the first layer by arranging the eggplants slices horizontally, sprinkle with parmesan, put in the mozzarella (cut into cubes), and finally pour some sauce, just enough to colour the surface

- Repeat the same procedure, this time placing the aubergines vertically. Finish the last layer in the same way.

- Preheat the oven to 180c (360 F). Place the dish on the middle shelf and cook for 25-30 minutes. Leave to cool for 10 minutes

- Enjoy

Mediterranean cuisine is full of healthy vegetable-based dishes. Palermo's caponata is one of these - a traditional dish prepared with aubergines, capers, tomato and olives.

Caponata Palermitana

Palermo style Caponata

Difficulty: *Medium*	Preparation: *Long*
Servings: *4*	Cost: *Low*

INGREDIENTS

- 500g eggplants
- 1 celery stick
- 100 tomato puree or peeled tomatoes
- 150g plum or cherry tomatoes half medium yellow onion
- 70g green olives
- 30g capers
- 2 tbsp white vinegar
- 2 tsp sugar
- 40g pine nuts
- Fresh basil leaves at your taste
- 15g raisins (optional)
- Oil for frying
- 2-3 tbsp olive oil

INSTRUCTIONS

- Start frying the aubergines. Peel them into 2-3 cm (1-inch) cubes. Heat plenty of oil in a large pan (about 170C 338F) and fry a few at a time until they're a nice golden colour

- Drain and place on absorbent paper to remove excess oil

- In some parts of Sicily, the caponata is made with peppers so you can add a couple of them with the aubergines

- Roughly chop the celery. Place it in a casserole dish and pour in some water, covering half of the celery

- Simmer on low heat until it's almost done, making sure the water has evaporated

- Pour in the olive oil and finely chopped onion

- Fry for a couple of minutes

- Rinse the capers and add them in

- Cut the olives in half and add them with the tomatoes and puree

- Season with salt and cook over a low heat for 10-15 minutes

- Add fried aubergines, basil leaves, pine nuts, vinegar and sugar.

- Season, mix well, and then remove the pan from the heat.

- Serve once cooled

Ribollita is one of the recipes that's traditionally associated with Tuscany: rustic and genuine. The Tuscan ribollita is a pleasure to eat, especially on cold winter nights. The essential ingredients for this are cannellini beans, black cabbage, cabbage, and stale bread.

INGREDIENTS

- 400g cannellini beans (dried or three tins)
- 200g black cabbage
- 200g chard
- Half medium white cabbage or cauliflower
- 1 carrot
- 1 garlic clove
- 1 yellow onion
- 1 celery stick
- 1-2 potatoes
- 200g peeled tomatoes
- 200g stale bread (sourdough)
- 3-4 tbsp olive oil
- Rosemary
- Black pepper

Ribollita Toscana

Tuscan Ribollita (boiled twice)

Difficulty: *Medium*   Preparation: *Long*

Servings: *6*   Cost: *Low*

INSTRUCTIONS

- Leave the dry beans in water overnight

- The day after, wash the beans

- Pour 2 litres of water in a pan. Add the beans, garlic and rosemary. Boil until beans are soft

- If you've used tinned beans, boil 800 ml of water and add three tins of beans with the liquid, garlic, salt and rosemary

- Cook for 10 minutes

- (the following steps are the same for tinned or untinned beans)

- Remove the rosemary (if it was a fresh stick) and the garlic

- Add salt at the end, to prevent hardening

- Put the olive oil in a casserole and finely cut a carrot, onion and celery. Cook on low-medium heat for about 3-5 minutes. Then add cut into cubes potatoes. Stir for a minute.

- Pour peeled tomatoes or puree. Stir. Drain the beans and leave them aside.

- Add the liquid into the casserole and put cut black cabbage. If you find the middle stalk too hard, cut it away. Cook for 30 minutes.

- Add cut cabbage or cauliflower (removing the cabbage stalk), chard and half of the beans

- Bring to boil, then reduce the heat

- Simmer for 20 minutes, stirring from time to time.

- Blend the remaining part of the beans.

- When the soup is ready, season with salt and pepper

- Add the blended beans and stir well

- Cut the stale bread into slices

- Place a few on the bottom of a pan and cover with a couple of ladles of soup

- Lay another layer of bread and cover with more soup, alternating the layers until you finish the ingredients

- Cover and cool to room temperature

- Place in the fridge for a couple of hours. Best if you cook this soup the day after

- Mix well. reheat and serve with a drizzle of olive oil. You can also add a sprinkle of chilli pepper and chilli oil.

- The dish is ready

DESSERT

Described as "One of history's most fortunate mistakes", the Cake dedicated to the beautiful island of Capri was born from an oversight. The baker forgot to add flour to a mix of walnut, almond, and chocolate. The dense and deep taste of the resulting mixture was irresistible, and gluten-free too!

Torta Caprese

Capri Cake

Difficulty: *Easy*	Preparation: *Short*
Servings: *10-12*	Cost: *Medium*

INGREDIENTS

- 230g dark chocolate (70% cocoa)
- 300g almond flour
- 170g butter room temperature
- 170 custard sugar
- 4 eggs
- Pinch of salt
- Icing sugar for dusting (24 cm/9-inch cake tin)

INSTRUCTIONS

- Melt the chopped chocolate with the butter in a water bath

- Let it melt over low heat, stirring to prevent it from sticking to the bottom

- Leave it aside to cook

- Divide the eggs into yolks and egg whites

- Whip the yolks with half of the sugar for a few minutes, until the mixture is fluffy and smooth.

- Add the melted chocolate to the yolk mixture

- Whip the mixture to make it smooth and velvety

- Add the almond flour, and mix with a spatula

- The mixture should be relatively compact and dense

- Beat the egg whites with the rest of the sugar. Transfer it into the mixture with the help of a spatula, mixing from the bottom-up to try and keep it fluffy

- Preheat the oven to 180 C (350 F) and select the static (conventional) function

- Bake it on the middle shelf for about 30-35 minutes (cooking times may vary from oven to oven, but remember the caprese must be moist inside)

- After 30 minutes, do the toothpick test - the crust should be formed, and the centre must be moist. Not wet, but humid.

- Leave it to cool for at least an hour

- If you turn the cake upside down too early, you risk breaking it. Run a palette or rounded knife around the inside edge of the cake tin and carefully turn the cake out onto a serving plate.

- To decorate the cake, place a fork on the cake's surface and sprinkle with icing sugar. Remove the cutlery gently.

Tiramisu is one of the most famous desserts in the world. A clever Maitresse of a brothel in Treviso created the recipe in 1800. Tiramisu means "pick me up". The lady offered her clients an aphrodisiac to reinvigorate them, and solve the problems they may have had with their conjugal duties on their return to their wives.

How much of this legend is true is still not known, but the dessert has stood the test of time.

The original recipe has raw eggs in it. If you want to be extra careful, you can beat the yolks at bath (bain-marie) to pasteurise them.

Eggs at bath or bain-marie or "bagnomaria"

PASTEURISE THE EGGS
• Take a stockpot (a) and a second pot or heatproof bowl (b) that should sit on it, not touching the water in (a)
• Bring the water almost to a boil, turn off the heat, whip the yolks with sugar for about 10-15 minutes. Use a hand mixer. It'll create a nice thick and clear mixture
• Work the mixture until it foams
• Fill the kitchen sink with a bit of cold water and immerse the bowl, leaving it there to cool
• Do the same with the egg whites
• If this is performed correctly, your eggs will be pasteurised

INGREDIENTS

- 4 fresh free-range eggs
- 140g castor sugar
- 500g mascarpone
- 400g ladyfingers (savoiardi biscuits)
- 350ml ready-made coffee. Sweetened to taste but not very sweet

Tiramisu

Tiramisu

Difficulty: *High*	Preparation: *Long*
Servings: *10*	Cost: *Medium*

INSTRUCTIONS

- Make half of the coffee and sweeten it to your taste

- You can use mocha (as in the original recipe) or espresso, diluted with boiled water, or instant coffee

- Add the rum and let it cool while you prepare the cream.

- Use eggs and mascarpone at room temperature (it will help them mix more smoothly)

- Beat the yolks and egg whites separately

- Beat the yolks with half of the sugar until it turns a light yellow colour

- Gradually add the mascarpone, gently folding it in. Add Marsala wine.

- Beat the egg whites with the remaining sugar until the mixture is firm, remembering to whip the egg whites well (there shouldn't be any trace of yolk in them)

- Add the egg whites to the mascarpone mixture a little at a time, mixing gently from top to bottom until creamy and well-combined

- Make sure you don't overdo it, or the mixture might become grainy

- Spread a generous spoonful of cream on the bottom of a 30x20cm baking dish

- Then dip the ladyfingers in sweetened cold coffee, first on one side and then on the other, but make sure it's a quick dip - if you soak them, the cake may collapse.

- Arrange the ladyfingers evenly on the cream, all in one direction

- Make a layer of mascarpone cream

- Continue to distribute the ladyfingers soaked in coffee, then make another layer of cream, spreading it evenly on the top with a spatula

- Cover the baking dish tightly with plastic wrap and refrigerate for a couple of hours, or even better, overnight

- Before serving, sprinkle your Tiramisu generously with unsweetened cocoa powder. You can use regular cocoa powder or the Dutch processed version

- Your Tiramisu is ready to be enjoyed.

This dessert is among the easiest and most delicious carnival sweets that are typical of Italian cuisine - soft as a cloud, fragrant and tasty.

You can enjoy carnival fritters on their own, or add raisins to the mixture.

To give a more original touch, you can enrich the aroma with grated ginger or a teaspoon of ground cinnamon.

Frittelle di Carnevale

Carnival Fritter

Difficulty: *Easy*   Preparation: *Short*

Servings: *25 pieces*   Cost: *Low*

INGREDIENTS

- 250g plain flour
- 75g castor sugar
- 100ml milk
- 2 eggs
- 1 sachet or one teaspoon of baking powder
- 30ml brandy
- 1 pinch salt
- Zest of half a lemon
- Zest of half an orange
- Sunflower or vegetable oil for frying
- Icing sugar

INSTRUCTIONS

- Beat the eggs with the sugar until the mixture has a light and foamy consistency

- Wash the lemon and orange, grate the zest and add to the egg and sugar mixture

- When you grate the lemon/orange rind, make sure you only scratch the outer rind without getting to the white, which would give your dough a bitter taste

- Stir in the milk (pouring it slowly, or a little at a time), a pinch of salt and brandy

- Stir well, then gradually add all the flour and baking powder, sifted and stirring thoroughly to avoid lumps

- Heat the oil in a large pan until it reaches 180 C, then dip in a spoonful of the mixture. Keep in mind these sweets are traditionally eaten in one bite

- Fry for a few minutes, turning the balls until they are well puffed and golden on all sides

- Drain with a slotted spoon and place them on a paper towel

- Sprinkle them with icing sugar

Italians are known to have fantastic family ties. When you see a recipe directly name one of the members more respected and loved, it has to mean something. Grandma's Cake is a timeless, simple, genuine classic of traditional Tuscan dessert. The one you can find on the tables of grandmothers on Sundays and consists of a crisp pastry shell, a soft filling of cream, garnished with toasted pine nuts and icing sugar.

A little trick, use icing sugar instead of sugar; it makes a smoother dough.

INGREDIENTS

For the crust:
- 2 yolk eggs
- 100g icing sugar
- 330g plain flour
- 200g cold butter
- 2 tbsp cold water
- Zest of one lemon

For the filling:
- 400ml full-fat milk
- 100ml single cream
- 6 yolk eggs
- 150g sugar
- 50g cornflour
- 1/3 vanilla pod or 1/2 tsp vanilla extract
- 22-24 cm in a fluted flan tin

Crostata della Nonna

Grandma's Cake

Difficulty: **Medium** Preparation: **Long**
Servings: **10-12** Cost: **Medium**

INSTRUCTIONS (CONT'D)

- Cut the flour, icing sugar, and cold butter from the fridge into small pieces.

- Put into the processor and blend until breadcrumbs form

- Add the yolks, zest and water into the processor. Make sure you only grate the outer rind of the lemon zest

- Once the dough has just started to form a ball, start kneading lightly to form a dough. Don't over-knead the pastry. Wrap in cling film and refrigerate for at least 30 minutes

- Meanwhile, make the custard. Put the milk and the seeds from a vanilla pod into a thick-bottomed saucepan. Heat it gently, but do not boil

- Pour the yolk and the sugar into the bowl, and mix. Add the cornflour and beat until well blended

- Remove the saucepan from the heat and pour the milk slowly into the egg mixture, whisking all the time with a balloon whisk

- Return the pan to a low heat, and gently stir with a spatula until thickened. Once ready, transfer the mixture to a low, wide baking dish and cover it with cling film

- Turn on the oven at 180 °C. Take the pastry out of the fridge. Divide it into 1/3 and 2/3 parts.

- Lightly dust the work surface with flour and roll out 2/3 part of the pastry. The dough is ready when it's a few centimetres wider than the pan you're using and 2-3 mm thick (you can spread the pastry between two sheets of baking paper to spread it more easily)

- Grease and flour the tin. Roll your pastry back onto a rolling pin, then gently unroll it on so it falls back onto the tart tin

- Press on the edges of the container and eliminate any excess dough. Prick the bottom with the tines of a fork

- Pour in the cooled custard

- Roll out the rest of the pastry into a disc to cover the cake completely. Pass the rolling pin over the tart tin and eliminate the excess edges, and prick the surface with the fork.

- Distribute the pine nuts over the surface by pressing lightly to make them stick to the pastry.

- Bake the cake in the medium-low part of the oven's static (conventional) function for the first 15 minutes at 180c then lower to 160c and cook slowly for another 45 minutes.

- The 'Crostata Della nonna' is ready when the surface is golden brown, it swells slightly (then lowers again) and the pine nuts are cooked but not toasted.

- Let it cool completely before sprinkling it with icing sugar.

Ricotta pie is a traditional Italian dessert from the Roman area. It's rich, tasty and easy to prepare, with a crumbly pastry base and a soft filling of ricotta cream and raisins.

INGREDIENTS

- 300g plain flour
- 130g cold butter
- 140g custard sugar
- 1 egg
- 2 egg yolks
- Zest of 1/2 lemon
- A pinch of salt
- 500g ricotta
- 60 g sugar
- 1 egg
- 1 egg yolk
- 50g raisins
- 30ml rum (or brandy)
- Zest of 1/2 lemon
- Zest of 1/2 orange
- A pinch of cinnamon
- 22-24 cm pie plate or tart tin
- (Optional) Chocolate chips 50g or candied fruit 50g
- candied fruit 50g

Crostata di Ricotta

Ricotta Cake Roman Style

Difficulty: *High*	Preparation: *Long*
Servings: *10-12*	Cost: *Medium*

INSTRUCTIONS

- Soak the raisins in the rum and let them rest while you prepare the shortcrust pastry

- Cut the flour, sugar, a pinch of salt and cold butter into small pieces and put into a processor

- Blend until you have breadcrumbs

- Add the yolks, egg, lemon and orange zests into the processor

- When you grate the lemon and orange rind, make sure you only scratch the outer rind without getting to the white, which would give your dough a bitter taste

- Once the dough has started to form a ball, turn out onto a work surface and knead lightly. Don't over-knead the pastry, as this gives the pastry a hard texture

- Wrap in cling film and refrigerate for at least 30 minutes

- While the pastry rests, prepare the ricotta filling.

- If there is any liquid in ricotta, drain it

- Pour the ricotta into a bowl with the egg yolks, egg and sugar

- Mix well to obtain a smooth, creamy texture

- Mix the raisins together with the liqueur, zests and cinnamon

- Add chocolate chips or candied fruit (optional)

- After 30 minutes, turn on the oven at 180 °C.

- Take 3/4 of the dough and roll it out to a thickness of half of cm. Try to give it a round shape

- Take a pie plate, oil it and dust it with flour, then line it with the pastry circle that you've rolled out and prick it with a fork

- Leave the excess dough hanging over the edge

- Pour in the ricotta cream, and turn the left edge towards the inside of the pan

- Prepare strips with the remaining parts of the pastry, and spread them over the cream, intertwining them in a diamond pattern or a crossed-hatch pattern

- Bake in the lower part of the oven for 40-50 minutes a5t 180 °C.

- Once cooked, the pastry should have a golden colour

- Let the cake cool to room temperature and sprinkle it with icing sugar

- Enjoy it! And if you are lucky to have some leftovers, the next day flavour is even better!

Printed in Great Britain
by Amazon